MW00914274

A Bouquet
of Herbs

Photography and Design
By Koren Trygg
Text By Lucy Poshek

ANTIOCH GOURMET
GIFT BOOKS

Published by Antioch Publishing Company
Yellow Springs, Ohio 45387

ISBN 0-89954-829-6

A BOUQUET OF HERBS

Printed and bound in the U.S.A.

CONTENTS

A HISTORY OF HERBS

Herbs have been used in cooking, medicine, cosmetics, perfumes, magical practices, and even embalming for nearly five thousand years.

Ancient civilizations believed that gods and spirits dwelled in trees and plants, so all herbs were thought to contain either protective or harmful mystical powers. As plants and herbs were the only medicines then in use, the first physicians were also the first botanists. Early Greek herbals, which listed the curative properties of hundreds of plants, influenced the study of medicine for many centuries.

Botanical interest came to a peak during the Middle Ages, a time also known as the golden age of herbalism. Herb gardens were found at every English monastery and castle. Still rooms were used daily for the concoction of herbal cordials, cosmetics, seasonings and remedies. Household cooks used herbs and flowers liberally, often distributing ten to twenty different varieties in one dish. And since refrigeration did not yet exist, herbs were also used to preserve meats and mask the bad taste of tainted foods.

Before the days of regular bathing, herbs were also valued as air purifiers. Sweet-smelling plants such as lavender, marjoram, and mint were frequently strewn on the

floors to freshen the fetid air and deter fleas. Sprigs of rosemary, sage and thyme, known for their antiseptic properties, were burned in sick rooms and carried around to help fend off the plague.

When the European immigrants settled in America during the seventeenth century, they brought their favorite herb seeds with them. There, they were also introduced to the culinary and healing values of native herbs used by the American Indians.

Herbal use went through a general decline during the eighteenth and nineteenth centuries, however, as the scientific knowledge of newly industrialized nations increased, man-made drugs were invented, and gardening space dwindled. But in the countryside and less "progressive" nations, the use of herbs never waned.

The last thirty years have seen a revival of herbal interest everywhere. People are now looking for natural alternatives to overly-processed foods, medicines, and cosmetics. The use of fresh, natural flavorings and light dishes—the basis of *nouvelle cuisine*—is here to stay. And, as the redolent scent of herbs is said to alleviate stress in our ever-more hectic world, we are also rediscovering their uses in aromatherapy.

The benefits of herbal remedies are once more being recognized as new studies reveal that there may be some sprigs of truth to those old wives' tales about herbs after all.

TYPES OF HERBS–
THEIR USES AND LORE

BASIL

Of all the culinary herbs, basil is perhaps the best loved. There are many kinds of basils—lemon, sacred, lettuce-leaf, anise, cinnamon, spice and Italian Genoa green, to name a few. Purple-leafed Dark Opal basil is extremely ornamental, whereas sweet basil is found most often commercially.

In Italy, basil has always been associated with love, as a token of romance, and certainly no Italian dish is complete without it. Its sweet, clove-like fragrance has a special

affinity with tomatoes, green salads, eggs, sauces and soups. Basil is also the base for pesto sauce. The leaves and white flowers are an ideal flavoring for oil or vinegar and as a garnish.

If a girl wears a sprig of basil in Italy, it means her beau no longer has to keep his distance.

BAY
Because the bay laurel tree was presumably sacred to the Greek god Apollo, it became customary to crown victorious athletes, poets, warriors and emperors with wreaths of bay leaves—thus, the expression "to win one's laurels."

In cookery, the bay leaf is indispensable as a savory addition to sauces, meats, bouquets garnis, fish, soups, and stews. Use with discretion—one leaf is enough to flavor a dish for six people.

CILANTRO
Also called Chinese parsley and coriander—the seeds of the herb are the spice known as coriander—the chopped fresh leaves of cilantro have a clean, concentrated flavor that is frequently used in Southwestern, Mexican, Middle Eastern and Oriental dishes. Cilantro adds a refreshing pungency to salsa, fajitas, vegetables, and green salads.

DILL

The feathery leaves and slightly tart taste of dill make it both an attractive garnish and popular flavoring, whether fresh or dried. Dill complements cucumbers, sour cream, yogurt, cole slaw, potatoes, fish, poultry and vegetables. The seeds are good in vinegar and wonderful for pickling.

Dill served as a medicine for Egyptian doctors five thousand years ago. Considered a soothing herb (the Norse word "dilla" means "to lull"), dill was also much used by early Scandinavians to induce sleep and cure nervous conditions. The herb is still immensely popular in Scandinavia—on their famous open-faced sandwiches—and in Eastern Europe.

FENNEL

All parts of fennel—the seeds, leaves and flowers—have a licorice flavor which goes well with salads, artichokes, vegetables, fish, poultry, potatoes, apple pies, marinara sauce, soups and stews. The Italians eat the entire plant as a vegetable. Common, or Sweet, and Florence, or Finnocchio, are the two major fennel varieties. Florence fennel, with its swollen, vegetable-like base, has a slightly milder flavor.

Fennel has long been lauded for promoting longevity and strengthening the eyesight. Also considered an appetite suppressor, fennel was eaten in the Middle Ages to relieve the pangs of hunger.

The leaves of fennel are best used fresh, as they do not dry well.

LAVENDER

The fresh, long-lasting perfume of lavender, especially the English variety, has long made it popular in sachets, potpourri and cosmetics. The scent of the flowers is said to calm the nerves and relieve headaches. Lavender was once used liberally in the kitchen (lavender conserve was a favorite of Queen Elizabeth I), but the perfumed flowers are added only rarely now to salads, desserts and fruits such as berries.

Lavender should be cut just before the flowers are fully open, hung upside down for a few days, then rubbed down to remove the flowers. It is a lovely old custom to set out bowls of the flowerheads in which to dip the fingers.

MARJORAM AND OREGANO

Among the confusing varieties of marjorams—all members of the *Origanum* genus—are pot marjoram, sweet marjoram, and oregano. Oregano and sweet marjoram are favored for cooking.

Sweet marjoram casts a fresh, spicy fragrance over the Mediterranean hills where it grows wild. It is still used often in perfumes today. A symbol of honor and happiness, the herb was once woven into bridal crowns. The scented crushed leaves were also a favorite strewing herb.

Oregano, also known variously as common marjoram, wild marjoram, winter marjoram, and Mexican sage, is most often used dried in Italian and tomato dishes, pizza, chicken, vegetables, eggs and meats. Both the marjorams and oregano should be reserved for robust-flavored dishes.

1. *Italian Parsley*

2. *Fennel*

3. *Parsley*

4. *Sage*

5. *Bay*

6. *Marjoram*

7. *Rosemary*

8. *Cilantro*

9. *Oregano*

10. *Dill*

11. *Basil*

12. *Tarragon*

13. *Mint*

14. *Lavender*

15. *Thyme*

MINT

There are many different kinds of mint: curly, apple, orange, lemon, pineapple, chocolate, peppermint, spearmint, ginger, field, Asian, pennyroyal and catnip, to name a few. Peppermint and spearmint are the two best-known varieties.

Spearmint, considered an aid to digestion, is a traditional accompaniment to lamb, either as a mint jelly or sauce. It also goes well with cream cheese, carrots and peas. French cooks often steam fresh garden peas with a leaf of fresh lettuce and a few fresh mint leaves for a savory summer dish.

Mint leaves and their edible flowers add a cool taste and rich green garnish to fruit, teas, juleps and chocolate.

PARSLEY

Not only is parsley high in iron and Vitamins A and C, but it also has the breath-freshening power to neutralize the scent of garlic and onion. The mild taste of parsley makes it a good blending agent for other herbs. A most universal seasoning and garnish, parsley can be added to just about any non-dessert food.

Many different varieties of curly-leafed and flat-leafed parsley exist, and one of them—the Hamburg parsley—is eaten like a vegetable. Although some curly-leafed varieties are showier, Italian parsley is one of the most flavorful. Parsley is often used as a salad green in Middle Eastern cooking and as a ubiquitous garnish in America.

ROSEMARY

Rosemary is a Mediterranean coastal evergreen plant that has an ancient history of uses: as a garland in early Greece and Rome; as a strewing herb and protection against the plague in medieval times; and for bridal wreaths during Shakespeare's day. Rosemary was thought to stimulate the memory and relieve headaches.

The stiff, needle-like leaves of rosemary have a resinous, camphor taste similar to pine needles. A potent seasoning, rosemary leaves and sprigs are used sparingly in marinades, stuffings, with meat, pork, poultry, and vegetables. A rosemary branch dipped in oil makes a savory basting brush for grilled meats and vegetables. The leaves are also tasty on breads.

SAGE

Sage, synonymous for wisdom, was once used to preserve the wit, memory and longevity. Known to have antiseptic properties, it was popular as a strewing herb in early times. The belief that burning sage leaves like incense will cleanse a room of bad feelings still endures today.

The musky, assertive taste of sage—garden sage is the best-known variety—has made it a traditional American and English seasoning for stuffings, sausages, pork, chowders, poultry, and breads. Fresh sage is much preferable to dried. In Switzerland, young sage leaves are dipped in batter and fried to make "little mice."

TARRAGON

Tarragon is of the *Artemisia* genus, which includes some of the most aromatic herbs. Native to Siberia, tarragon means "little dragon" in French, in reference to the coiled shape of its roots.

Of the French and Russian varieties of tarragon, French has the better flavor. It is used much in French cooking: in Béarnaise and mustard sauces, salad dressings, *fines herbes*, bouquets garnis, with eggs, mushrooms, artichokes, tomatoes, and chicken. (Try roast chicken on a bed of tarragon sprigs.) Tarragon has the ability to remove fishy odors and is a principal ingredient in tartar sauce. The practice of steeping tarragon in white wine vinegar goes back to the sixteenth century.

THYME

Lemon, caraway, orange, and camphor thyme are only a few of the countless varieties of this spicy, slightly sweet Mediterranean herb. Both the leaves and edible flowers of thyme are used in sauces, bouquets garnis, stews, stuffings, honey, chowders, creole dishes, with poultry, fish, pork, and potatoes. In fact, thyme enhances any food but dessert, and makes a handsome garnish as well.

Known to have antiseptic properties, thyme was a favorite strewing herb and is still the basis for some mouthwashes and cough medicines. Lemon thyme is considered a soothing herb for head cushions.

"I know a bank whereon the wild thyme blows."
WILLIAM SHAKESPEARE

18

PRESERVING HERBS

There is no lovelier sight in a kitchen than bunches of aromatic herbs and flowers hanging from the rafters. The earthy textures and fresh scents of drying lavender, marjoram and rosemary can bring a rustic country garden into the most urban kitchen. **Air-drying** herbs is a tradition that had endured for centuries, and it is still the most enjoyable way to preserve herbs.

To air-dry herbs: Rinse the leaves and pat thoroughly dry with a paper towel. Bundle the herbs together with rubber bands so they won't fall out when they shrink. Hang them upside down in a cool, airy place. They will take from several days to two weeks to dry. If left hanging too long, they will turn brown and lose their flavor.

Rose petals, herb flower blossoms, and large-leafed herbs (cut them from the stalk or they will mold) are best dried on a well-ventilated screen in a dark place to preserve their color. Turn the petals and leaves daily. They should be crisp in several days, but if not, place them in a cool oven until dry.

Dried herbs should ideally be stored in light-proof, tightly-closed bottles and kept in a cool place. They will last for up to a year.

Fresh herbs will last a week if you **refrigerate** them in a jar one-third full of water, the tops covered with a plastic bag. Some herbs can also be **frozen** in plastic bags and kept for six to eight months.

"Lavender, sweet blooming Lavender,
Six bunches a penny to-day.
Lavender, sweet blooming Lavender,
Ladies, buy it while you may."

OLD LONDON STREET CRY

POTPOURRI

Like strewing herbs, early potpourris were used to sweeten fetid rooms. Containing antiseptic herbs—rosemary, lavender, sage—mixed with spices, oils and fixatives, they were left in a closed container to decompose into a moist mixture. "Potpourri," in fact, translates as "rotten pot."

Potpourri today is usually a dry mixture of sweet-smelling dried flowers and petals with aromatic herbs, seeds and spices, a fixative, and sometimes essential oils and spirits.

Tips on Making Potpourri:

—Flowers and herbs must be dried to preserve their color and scent.

—Flower blossoms that aren't yet fully open are best for drying because they contain the most essential oils.

—Roses such as wild dog, sweet briar, eglantine, cabbage, and tuberoses are traditionally used in potpourri because they are less likely to lose their fragrance after drying. Other good flowers include violets, summer flowering jasmine, lily of the valley, lavender, red bergamot, chamomile, cassia, and rose geranium.

—To add bulk to potpourri, include brightly colored, yet unscented, dried flowers and buds such as larkspur, marigolds and grape hyacinth.

—The best herbs to use in potpourri are sage, bay, lemon balm, the mints, bergamot, rosemary, and lemon verbena leaves.

—Among the favorite potpourri spices are coriander and caraway seeds, nutmeg, cloves, cinnamon, ginger, allspice and mace, anise and tonka or vanilla beans. One tablespoon of powdered spices is enough for two to five cups of potpourri.

—After the dried flowers, herbs and spices are mixed, a fixative must be added. Fixatives, which slow down evaporation of the essential oils, include common and sea salt, powdered orris root, dried orange peel, and gum benzoin. The usual measure is one tablespoon of fixative to every two to five cups of potpourri.

—A drop or two of essential oil, such as rosemary, geranium, lavender, rose, peppermint, and bergamot can also be added to strengthen the scent. Dried, grated orange or lemon peel is optional.

—There are many recipes for potpourri, but it is more fun to experiment with your favorite flowers and herbs, creating a personal scent.

To Make Potpourri: Mix the dried herbs and flowers together in an earthenware jar and add essential oils. Seal for one to six weeks, shaking and stirring every day or two. Then place in clear glass or china bowls or jars.

Cover the mixture when you expect to be away for awhile. To revive tired potpourri, add a drop of essential oil, brandy, olive oil, alcohol, or lemon juice and stir.

Lavender Potpourri

1 cup (8 fl. oz.) dried lavender flowers
¾ cup (6 fl. oz.) dried rose petals
½ cup (4 fl. oz.) dried marjoram leaves
¼ cup (2 fl. oz.) each dried mint and thyme leaves
1 tbsp. (¾ Br. tbsp.) orris root powder or dried
  orange peel
¼ tsp. each ground cloves and cinnamon
few drops lavender oil

*Note: You can substitute the lavender oil with rose
geranium oil or even oil from a soft bath bead.*

HERBAL SACHETS AND PILLOWS

Over the ages, sachets have
been used for perfuming closets, drawers, pockets, books,
and writing paper. They can also be tied to chairbacks
and bedposts, or tucked under sofa and chair pillows.
They are usually made with heavily-scented herbs—lavender, rosemary, rose, basil, lemon verbena, the thymes,
marjorams and mints—but also with milder spices, such as
caraway and coriander. These herbs are strong enough to
last without a fixative, but a little dried orange or lemon
peel is sometimes added, nonetheless.

To Make a Sachet: Sachets can be made with either one herb, such as lavender, or with any potpourri mixture. Sew cotton lawn or organdy into little bags or pillow squares. Fill them with your preferred mixture, then tie with ribbon or sew them up with lace edging. To enhance their fragrance, sprinkle several drops of essential oil onto a piece of flannel and place this in the stuffing. Periodically squeeze the sachets when their perfume fades.

~ ~ ~

In the early days, bedstraw mattresses were stuffed with lavender to provide a calming scent for bedtime. Head pillows, an attractive, modern alternative, provide soothing, natural remedies for headaches and tension.

Since they rest close to the face, head pillows don't need the potent spices and oils that sachets contain. The primary herbs used are peppermint, sage, lemon balm, roses, and lavender. Secondary herbs include dill, thyme, chamomile, marjoram, rosemary, bergamot, lemon verbena, woodruff, and rosemary (the last two are known for their sleep-inducing properties).

To Make an Herbal Pillow: Sew a piece of muslin on three sides and most of the fourth. Stuff the pillow with scented herbs, or, for a milder fragrance, one cup herbs and the rest fiberfill. Sew up the fourth side. Make an outer slip cover out of any lightweight cotton, linen or silk material that allows the scent to pass through.

HERBAL AROMATHERAPY

Just as ingesting some herbs can produce certain effects, so can inhaling their aroma. Some herbal aromas have the ability to comfort, soothe, heal, beautify, and stimulate. When the scent of dried herbs or herbal oils are used deliberately for such purposes, it is called aromatherapy.

There are many ways to disperse herbal aromas. The early colonists perfumed their homes by simply throwing herbs and spices in a pot of simmering water. Here are some other easy methods:

Infusion—Pour two cups boiling water over one-half cup of herbs, let steep for ten to twenty minutes, and strain through a paper filter. Infusions are most effective when added to the bath or inhaled from a basin of hot water.

You can also wrap dried herbs in a cheesecloth or tea infuser and steep in a pot, basin or bath of hot water. This way, the herbs can be re-used several times.

Decoction—Same as an infusion except that you add the herbs to cold water first and then bring to a boil. A decoction is slightly stronger than an infusion.

Essential Oils—These are the highly concentrated essences of herbs and flowers. Only three to six drops of essential oil should be used at one time—on a tissue to be

directly inhaled, diluted in vegetable oils for massage or perfume, sprinkled in the carpet to freshen a room, or in the bath water.

Aromatic Effects of Herbs

Rosemary stimulates the nervous system and clears the head. Clary sage produces a sense of euphoria for some people. Basil refreshes the mental powers. Rose is romantic and exciting to the senses.

Peppermint calms the stomach when inhaled just as fennel does when ingested. Since peppermint contains natural cooling menthol, it is also soothing in the bath for aching muscles.

A few drops of lavender oil (the only essential oil which can be used directly on the skin) rubbed into the nape of the neck or sprinkled in the bath helps to calm the nerves and promote sleep. Marjoram is another powerful sedative aroma.

Other oils, when diluted in water or oil, can help beautify the skin and hair. A thyme-and-water infusion, for example, makes a refreshing skin toner. An antiseptic lavender and bergamot tonic helps clear up oily skin. Rosemary and thyme are natural enhancers for all types of hair.

"There's rosemary, that's for remembrance; pray you, love, remember."

WILLIAM SHAKESPEARE

CULINARY TIPS

Not so long ago, it was customary to restrict **kitchen herbs** to cooking, **salad herbs** to salads, and **perfumed herbs** to potpourri. Now, there are no set rules. We can throw flower petals in our salads, salad herbs in our hot dishes, and cooking herbs in our potpourri.

However, there are a few general culinary guidelines which remain constant:

—With few exceptions, fresh herbs are best. Basil, bor-

age, parsley, chives, chervil, cilantro, burnet, summer savory and tarragon all have very pungent flavors that are practically nonexistent when dried.

—Before adding fresh or dried herbs to a dish, crush them in your hand or pulverize them with a mortar to release the flavorful oils.

—When substituting dried herbs for fresh, use ⅓ teaspoon powdered or ½ teaspoon crushed herbs for every tablespoon of fresh chopped herbs.

—Delicately-flavored herbs should be added to hot dishes at the last minute or their flavor will be lost. For cold foods, however, the opposite is true—the sooner they are seasoned, the better.

—To reduce herbs to a powder, use a mortar and pestle or the back of a wooden spoon.

—Choose one dominant herb, adding others in smaller amounts. Strongly-flavored herbs such as tarragon, lovage, sage and rosemary are best not used together.

—Herbs such as thyme, rosemary, tarragon and marjoram are good salt replacers. Sweet cicely, angelica, lemon balm and lemon thyme serve well as sugar substitutes.

"Tarragon...is one of the most agreeable of salads, which requires neither salt nor vinegar, for it possesses the taste of these two condiments."

RUELLIUS
(botanist, 1536)

BOUQUETS GARNIS

Also called "herb bouquets," **bouquets garnis** are a blend of herbs that are used to flavor soups, stews and braised dishes, to be removed after cooking.

Classic fresh bouquets garnis include one bay leaf, three sprigs of thyme, one sprig of tarragon and two sprigs of parsley. But you can play with the proportions, or use dried herbs, or feature another herb altogether. For chicken or fish, try adding a sprig or two of dill or fennel leaves, lovage or celery leaves, and cracked peppercorns. For lamb or pork, try a sprig of rosemary. Basil works well with beef.

To make bouquets garnis: place the herb mixture in the center of a 3- or 4-inch cheesecloth square and tightly bind the edges together with a string. You may want to make a batch of bouquets at one time and store them in a tightly-covered container.

A tea ball also provides an easily removable container for bouquets garnis.

"The composition of bouquets garnis is a matter so grave that its different constituents should be weighed on jeweler's scales and counted out in karats, like diamonds."
D'AIGREFEUILLE

Herbal Vinegars & Oils

Tarragon Vinegar: 4 fresh tarragon sprigs
2 cups (16 fl. oz.) white wine vinegar
Oregano Vinegar: 4 fresh oregano sprigs
2 cups (16 fl. oz.) white wine vinegar
Sage Vinegar: 4 fresh sage sprigs
2 cups (16 fl. oz.) white wine vinegar
Basil Oil: 10 fresh basil leaves
2 cups (16 fl. oz.) olive oil

Fill a jar with herbs and liquid. Place jar in a sunny spot for 2 to 4 weeks, shaking now and then.

Sage Fritters

¾ cup (6 fl. oz.) flour
¼ tsp. salt
1 ½ tbsp. (1 Br. tbsp.) olive oil

1 large egg, separated
½ cup (4 fl. oz.) water
20-25 sage leaves

Two hours ahead: Sift flour into bowl. Add salt, olive oil, egg yolk, water, and 1 tsp. (¾ Br. tsp.) chopped sage leaves pressed through a garlic press. Stir until smooth. Let stand covered in cool place for 2 hours.

While heating up oil in pan, beat egg white until stiff. Fold into batter. Rub each sage leaf slightly with the fingers to release the volatile oils before dipping into the batter. Deep-fry the leaves until golden brown and drain them on paper towels. Serves 4 as an appetizer.

Pesto Bread
Pesto Sauce:

1 ½ cups (12 fl. oz.) fresh basil leaves
1 cup (8 fl. oz.) fresh parsley leaves
½ cup (4 fl. oz.) olive oil
2 garlic cloves
1 tsp. (¾ Br. tsp.) salt
½ cup (4 fl. oz.) freshly grated Parmesan cheese
¼ cup (2 fl. oz.) pine nuts or walnuts (opt.)

Purée the basil, parsley, oil, pine nuts, garlic and salt in a blender or food processor. Stir in Parmesan cheese.

Bread:

1 package dry yeast
1 cup (8 fl. oz.) warm water
¾ tsp. salt
1½ tsp. (1 Br. tsp.) sugar
3 cups (24 fl. oz.) all purpose flour

Place the flour in a bowl and warm it in the oven for a few minutes while it preheats to 400°F. In a separate bowl, dissolve yeast in warm water. Add sugar, salt, and then the warmed flour, cup by cup. Turn out the bread and knead until elastic. Place in oiled bowl and let rise about 1 hour.

Punch dough down and roll out on a flat surface with a rolling pin. Spread pesto sauce evenly over dough to desired thickness (leftover pesto can be stored in refrigerator with thin film of olive oil on top) and roll it up. Place it in a crescent shape on a cookie sheet sprinkled with cornmeal. Allow to rise for 5 minutes. Place pan of boiling water in bottom of oven and bake bread for 25 minutes or until golden brown. Slice before serving so that layers of pesto are displayed.

It is a Mediterranean belief that the planting of basil must be accompanied by cursing for it to flourish.

Shown clockwise from top left:
Rosemary-Garlic Focaccia,
Herbed Vegetable Soup,
Pesto Bread, and Fines Herbes Butter

Rosemary-Garlic Focaccia

Bread:

2 packages yeast
2 cups (16 fl. oz.) warm water
2 tbsp. (1½ Br. tbsp.) sugar
¾ cup (6 fl. oz.) olive oil
1 tsp. (¾ Br. tsp.) salt
5½ cups (44 fl. oz.) white flour

Topping:

1½ cloves minced garlic
2 tbsp. (1½ Br. tbsp.) olive oil
1½ tbsp. (1 Br. tbsp.) dried rosemary leaves
1½ tsp. (1 Br. tsp.) kosher salt

Dissolve yeast in warm, not hot, water. Add sugar, oil and salt. Mix in flour until dough is smooth but still sticky. Place dough in a greased bowl and let rise twice, punching down after each rise.

Oil a 15- x 10- x 1-inch pan and press dough evenly out to the edges. Let rise in a warm place until almost double in bulk.

Before baking, dimple the dough slightly with your fingertips, brush it with 2 tbsp. (1½ Br. tbsp.) oil, and sprinkle with garlic, rosemary and salt. Place pan in the lower half of the oven and bake at 375°F for 30 minutes or until golden brown. Serve warm. (Leftover focaccia makes good sandwich bread when split.)

Herbed Vegetable Soup

6 tbsp. (4½ Br. tbsp.) extra virgin olive oil
4 large cloves garlic, minced
2 stalks celery, diced
½ tsp. dried thyme leaves
1 28-oz. can Italian-style tomatoes, crushed
6 fresh basil leaves, chopped
6 cups (48 fl. oz.) vegetable broth
½ tsp. dried *fines herbes*
½ cup (4 fl. oz.) pearl barley
4 red potatoes, diced
2 medium carrots, diced
2 sprigs fresh marjoram
1 cup (8 fl. oz.) water
2 cups (16 fl. oz.) shredded green cabbage
1 small zucchini, diced
1 6-oz. can of corn
1 15-oz. can red kidney beans with liquid
salt and pepper to taste
grated Monterey Jack cheese (opt.)

Heat olive oil in an 8-quart pot. Add garlic and celery, and sauté over medium heat for 5 minutes. Add dried thyme leaves and cook 2 minutes more. Add canned tomatoes with liquid, fresh basil, vegetable broth, and fines herbes. *Stir in the barley, red potatoes, carrots, and fresh marjoram. Bring to a boil. Reduce heat, cover, and simmer 20 minutes. Remove fresh marjoram sprigs. Stir in 1 cup water. Add cabbage, zucchini, corn, and red kidney beans. Salt and pepper to taste. Simmer uncovered 10 to 15 minutes until vegetables are tender. Garnish if desired with Jack cheese.*

Fines Herbes Butter

Fines herbes are a classic blend of four herbs—parsley, chervil, chives, and tarragon—finely minced in equal amounts. They are frequently used in French dishes and can be found dried and pre-mixed in gourmet shops.

To make fines herbes butter: Cut 4 oz. slightly softened butter into pieces. Beat or blend butter with 3 tbsp. (2¼ Br. tbsp.) fines herbes and 1 tbsp. (¾ Br. tbsp.) lemon juice until smooth. Chill until firm.

Tomato-Cucumber Salad

1 cup (8 fl. oz.) cubed tomatoes
1 cup (8 fl. oz.) diced cucumbers
½ cup (4 fl. oz.) fresh parsley leaves, cut up
½ cup (4 fl. oz.) black olives
¼ cup (2 fl. oz.) chopped red onions

Serve on a bed of greens.

Dill Dressing

½ cup (4 fl. oz.) light sour cream
½ cup (4 fl. oz.) plain yogurt
½ cup (4 fl. oz.) cubed cucumbers, peeled and seeded
½ tsp. dried dill
salt to taste

Serves 4.

Shown from top:
Tomato-Cucumber Salad with
Dill Dressing and
Grilled Shrimp with Cilantro Sauce

Fennel Marinara Sauce

3 medium garlic cloves or
  shallots, minced
2 tsp. (1½ Br. tsp.) fennel
  seeds, ground well with
  mortar and pestle
3 bay leaves

1 32-oz. can stewed tomatoes
dash of liquid smoke (opt.)
2 tbsp. (1½ Br. tbsp.) pine
  nuts (opt.)
grated mozzarella or
  Parmesan cheese

Brown garlic in oil. Mix in tomatoes, fennel, bay leaves, and liquid smoke. Let simmer for 15 minutes. Meanwhile, brown pine nuts in a small ungreased pan.

Before serving, remove bay leaves. Spoon onto cooked pasta, with pine nuts and a sprinkling of cheese on top. Serves 4.

Grilled Shrimp with Cilantro Sauce

2 lbs. raw jumbo shrimp,
  shelled and de-veined
melted butter for grilling
½ lb. butter
juice of one small lime

3 cups (24 fl. oz.) cilantro
  (stems removed), puréed
3 large garlic cloves, minced
¼-½ tsp. cayenne powder or
  flakes

Brush shrimp with melted butter and grill until cooked. Meanwhile, place ½ lb. butter in saucepan over low heat. Add lime juice, cilantro, garlic, and cayenne powder. Mix together until butter is melted. Dip grilled shrimp in sauce. Serves 4-6.

Chicken Tarragon

1 lb. boneless, skinless chicken breasts
12 medium mushrooms, sliced thickly
3 tbsp. (2¼ Br. tbsp.) butter or oil
1 cup (8 fl. oz.) chicken stock
1 tbsp. (¾ Br. tbsp.) fresh chopped tarragon
1 tbsp. (¾ Br. tbsp.) fresh chopped parsley
¼ cup (2 fl. oz.) Drambuie or white wine
2 tbsp. (1½ Br. tbsp.) cornstarch mixed with ¼ cup
   (2 fl. oz.) water
1 tbsp. (¾ Br. tbsp.) capers
salt and fresh ground pepper to taste

Pound chicken breasts briefly so that their thickness is more evenly distributed. Roll them in finely blended oatmeal (or flour). Lightly brown chicken in 2 tbsp. (1½ Br. tbsp.) butter, then remove to plate. Add 1 tbsp. (¾ Br. tbsp.) butter to pan and lightly sauté mushrooms. Set them aside with the chicken.

Using same pan, mix chicken stock, Drambuie, capers, tarragon, and parsley together, bringing to a boil. Stir in cornstarch mixture until sauce is thickened. Pour sauce over chicken and top with mushrooms. Serves 4.

*"Parsley—the jewel of herbs,
both in the pot and on the plate."*

ALBERT STOCKLI

43

Fillet of Sole in Packets

4 to 6 stalks celery, cut in ¼-inch dice
2 leeks (white portion only), cut in ¼-inch dice
4 medium carrots, cut in ¼-inch dice
3 (or more) tbsp. (2¼ Br. tbsp.) butter
salt and freshly ground black pepper

2 lbs. fillets of sole
salt and freshly ground black pepper
2 ripe tomatoes, sliced
1 lemon, sliced
4 bay leaves
¾ tsp. fresh thyme, or ½ tsp. dried
4 squares (12 x 12 inches each) aluminum foil or
  parchment paper

*Preheat oven to 450°F. In a medium skillet, sauté
celery, leeks, and carrots in 3 or more tbsp. (2¼ Br.
tbsp.) butter, for 5 minutes, or until just tender. Sea-
son with salt and pepper.*

*On each foil or parchment square, layer one-fourth
of the ingredients in the following order: sautéed vegetables, sole fillets, salt and pepper, tomato slices,
lemon slices, bay leaf, thyme. Fold packets securely,
tucking edges under, and place on a baking sheet.
Bake 20 minutes.*

*Slit packets before serving, or allow guests to open
their own.*

Chocolate Mint Ice Cream De-Lite

2¼ cups (18 fl. oz.) lowfat milk
2 large eggs
1 tsp. (¾ Br. tsp.) vanilla extract
¼ cup (2 fl. oz.) sugar
4 tbsp. (3 Br. tbsp.) crème de menthe
2 tbsp. (1½ Br. tbsp.) cornstarch
¼ cup (2 fl. oz.) chocolate chips
fresh mint leaves for garnish

If the container of your ice cream maker needs to be placed in the freezer, be sure to do this well in advance. In a blender, mix 2 cups (16 fl. oz.) milk, eggs, vanilla, crème de menthe and sugar. Pour mixture into a saucepan. Heat slowly, stirring often. (Do not let mixture boil, or it will curdle.) In a glass measuring cup, whip cornstarch into remaining ¼ cup (2 fl. oz.) cool milk and add slowly to hot mixture, stirring constantly. Stir in chocolate chips until they are almost melted. When the mixture has a custard-like consistency, pour it immediately into a bowl. Cover and place in the refrigerator until chilled.

Pour chilled custard mixture into ice cream machine and make ice cream according to manufacturer's directions. Garnish with fresh mint leaves. Serves 4.

"The young sow wild oats. The old grow sage."
OLD PROVERB

GRAPHIC DESIGN BY GRETCHEN GOLDIE

PHOTO STYLING AND SETS BY SUE TALLON

PREPARED FOOD STYLED BY STEPHANIE PUDDY

ACKNOWLEDGMENTS

MONIKA BRANDL, DEBBIE & PAUL JOHANSSON,
STEVE LARWOOD, JOE POSHEK, MICHAEL THOMPSON,
ALVY, SOO LING, WOODY & HARRISON TRYGG; AND
SCENTSABILITIES AROMATHERAPY, STUDIO CITY, CA.
"FILLET OF SOLE IN PACKETS" FROM *CALIFORNIA FRESH*,
BY THE JUNIOR LEAGUE OF OAKLAND-EAST BAY